Gifts of Our People

An Alphabet of African American History

Portia George

Judson Press ® Valley Forge

Library of Congress Cataloging-in-Publication Data
George, Portia
     Gifts of our people: an alphabet of African American history/Portia George.
     p. cm.
     ISBN 0-8170-1228-1 (acid-free paper)
     1. Afro-Americans—History—Juvenile literature. 2. English language—Alphabet—Juvenile literature. [1. Afro-Americans—History.
2. Alphabet.] I. Title.
E185.G37 1995
920'.009296073—dc20
[B]
[E]   94-43706

Printed in the U.S.A.

96 97 98 99 00 01 02 03   9 8 7 6 5 4 3 2

To my parents, Florine and Leon Austin,
who instilled in their children the right to know God
and to use their God-given gifts and talents for his glory.

To my husband, Gary, and my son, Joel,
for their undying daily love, support, patience, and prayers,
without which this book would not be the success that it is.

To my sister, Flora,
for our wonderful grands Shakir and Nkosazana,
for whom this book was originally designed.

To my coworker Sally,
who has been my sounding board
from the first sketch to the finished product.

To all my family and friends,
"If I can help somebody with a word or song,
then my living shall not be in vain."

To our readers: "Being confident of this very thing,
that he which hath begun a good work in you will perform it
until the day of Jesus Christ" (Philippians 1:6, KJV).

Gifts of our People was created through the combined efforts of many at Judson Press, and I deeply appreciate their support. I want to say thanks to the editors, illustrators, designers, and my coworkers and friends.

Thanks also to all the other African American leaders, teachers, and authors, ordinary people who are trying to be positive role models for our children, helping their dreams be fulfilled and their accomplishments realized, showing them the way.

Architect, a person who designs buildings.

Julian Abele, born and educated in Philadelphia, was an architect who designed many important buildings, including the famed Philadelphia Museum of Art. Through his achievements he helped open doors for other African Americans in the field of architecture.

"For he looked for a city which hath foundations, whose builder and maker is God." (Hebrews 11:10)

 # Aa

Astronaut, a person who travels in a spacecraft.

Guion Stewart Bluford, Jr., became the first African American astronaut when he served as a crew member on the space shuttle *Challenger* in 1983.

"In the beginning God created the heaven and the earth." (Genesis 1:1)

Baseball, a game of ball played by two teams of nine in which four bases must be touched by a base runner in order to score a run.

Jackie Robinson became the first African American to play modern major league baseball when he joined the Brooklyn Dodgers in 1947.

"Thou shalt love thy neighbor as thyself."
(Leviticus 19:18)

 # Bb

Bicycle, a two-wheeled vehicle that one rides by sitting on a seat and pedaling with the feet.

I. R. Johnson invented the bicycle frame in 1899.

"Remember now thy creator in the days of thy youth."
(Ecclesiastes 12:1)

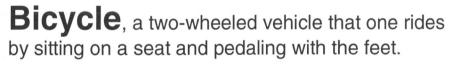

Church, a building made for public Christian worship.

George Liele, a slave preacher, organized one of the first African American churches between 1773 and 1775 in Silver Bluff, South Carolina.

"I was glad when they said unto me, Let us go into the house of the LORD." (Psalm 122:1)

 # Cc

Composer, a person who writes music.

Thomas Andrew Dorsey, a pianist, wrote hundreds of gospel songs and founded the National Convention of Gospel Choirs and Choruses in 1932.

"Sing forth the honour of his name." (Psalm 66:2)

Director, one who supervises the actors in a movie, a play, or a radio or TV show.

Oprah Winfrey is a well-known director-producer, actress, and international talk show host who regards her daily work as a ministry unto the Lord.

"In all thy ways acknowledge him, and he shall direct thy paths." (Proverbs 3:6)

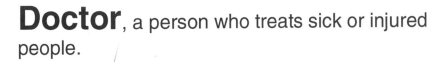 # Dd

Doctor, a person who treats sick or injured people.

Ben Carson overcame a difficult childhood to become a brilliant neurosurgeon. He made medical history in 1987 by successfully separating twins who had been joined at the head.

"I am the LORD that healeth thee." (Exodus 15:26)

Educator, one who helps a person grow in knowledge by teaching, instruction, or schooling.

Benjamin E. Mays was a preacher, a professor of mathematics and English, and the president of Morehouse College from 1940 to 1967.

"Study to show thyself approved unto God."
(2 Timothy 2:15)

Electric Railway, a railroad that operates over short distances and uses electricity as a source of power.

Granville T. Woods, an inventor of dozens of electrical devices, invented a telegraph system that prevented accidents on electric railways.

"I will cause thee to ride upon the high places of the earth . . . ." *(Isaiah 58:14)*

Filmmaker, a person who produces motion pictures.

John Singleton was the youngest person ever to be nominated for an Academy Award for best director and best screenplay, for his film *Boyz N the Hood.*

"Train up a child in the way he should go: and when he is old, he will not depart from it." (Proverbs 22:6)

Ff

Fountain Pen, a pen filled from an external source and containing an ink reservoir that automatically feeds into the point.

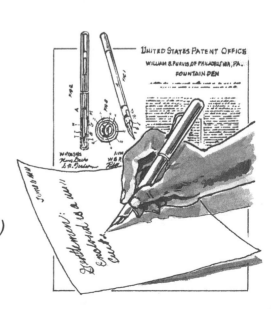

William B. Purvis improved the fountain pen by inventing an ink-feeding tube.

"What thou seest, write in a book . . . ." (Revelation 1:1)

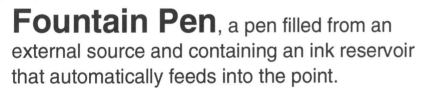

General, an officer of the highest rank in the United States Army.

Benjamin O. Davis, Sr., became the first African American to serve as a general in the United States army when he was named brigadier general in 1940.

"So didst thou lead thy people, to make thyself a glorious name." (Isaiah 63:14)

 # Gg

Golf Tee, a peg from which a golf ball is driven.

George F. Grant made improvements on the wooden golf tee.

"I will do all thy desire concerning timber of cedar, and concerning timber of fir." (1Kings 5:8)

Heart Surgeon, a doctor who performs operations on hearts.

Daniel Hale Williams was the first person in history to successfully operate on a human heart.

"Beloved, I wish above all things that thou mayest prosper and be in health, even as thy soul prospereth." (3 John 2)

  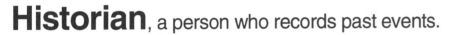

Hh

Historian, a person who records past events.

Carter G. Woodson, the father of black history, started the observance of Black History Week in 1926.

"Take thee a roll of a book, and write therein . . . ." (Jeremiah 36:2)

Inventor, a person who devises some new process, appliance, or machine.

Jan Ernst Matzeliger revolutionized the shoe industry in the United States in 1883 when he invented a machine that attached the upper leather part to the bottom part of the shoe.

"Loose thy shoe from off thy foot . . . ." *(Joshua 5:15)*

Ii

Ironing Board, a flat, cloth-covered board, often foldable and having legs, on which clothing is ironed.

Sarah Boone invented the ironing board in 1892, a device that is still used today.

"And he shall wash his clothes, and be clean . . . ." *(Leviticus 13:6)*

Journalist, one whose occupation is reporting, writing, editing, or broadcasting news.

Ida B. Wells Barnett fought against injustice in the late 1890s and was perhaps the most famous black female journalist in her time.

"It was needful for me to write unto you . . . ."
(Jude 1:3)

Jj

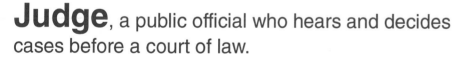

Judge, a public official who hears and decides cases before a court of law.

Thurgood Marshall became the first black member of the United States Supreme Court in 1967.

". . . Execute judgment and justice in the earth."
(Jeremiah 23:5)

Kentucky Derby, an annual horse race in Louisville, Kentucky.

Jimmy Winkfield was the winning jockey at the Kentucky Derby in 1901 and 1902.

"And they shall ride upon horses . . . ."
(Jeremiah 50:42)

Kk

Kwanzaa, an African American holiday, from December 26 until January 1, that honors African Americans and their history.

Maulana Ron Karenga, a professor of Pan-African studies and a black cultural leader, developed Kwanzaa as a holiday in 1966.

"Yea, happy is that people, whose God is the LORD."
(Psalm 144:15)

Lawn Mower, a machine used for cutting grass.

J. A. Burr invented the lawn mower in 1899.

"And God said, Let the earth bring forth grass . . . ."
(Genesis 1:11)

Ll

Lawyer, a person who advises or acts for clients in legal matters.

Edith Sampson, a lawyer and judge, was appointed by President Harry S. Truman as United States delegate to the United Nations in 1950.

"And the children of Israel came up to her for judgment." *(Judges 4:5)*

Mathematician, a person who is skilled in working with numbers.

Benjamin Banneker, a gifted inventor and mathematician, was one of the surveyors and planners appointed by George Washington to design the nation's capital.

"For unto this people shalt thou divide for an inheritance the land . . . ." (Joshua 1:6)

Mm

Missionary, a person who is sent to another place to teach and spread his or her faith.

Lott Carey, an ex-slave who purchased his freedom in 1813, was the first black missionary to West Africa and was governor of Liberia from 1828 to 1829.

"As my Father hath sent me, even so send I you. . . ." (John 20:21)

News Reporter, a person who gives accounts of current events.

Ed Bradley, co-anchor of the CBS news show *60 Minutes*, has won seven Emmy Awards for broadcast journalism.

"Whatsoever things are of good report . . . ." *(Philippians 4:8)*

 # Nn

Nobel Peace Prize, a prize awarded annually for achievement in the promotion of peace.

Dr. Martin Luther King, Jr., received the Nobel Peace Prize in 1964 for his nonviolent leadership of the civil rights movement.

"If it be possible, as much as lieth in you, live peaceably with all men." *(Romans 12:18)*

Olympic Games, a sport competition held every four years for athletes from all over the world.

Jesse Owens won four gold medals in track and field at the 1936 Olympics.

"And rejoiceth as a strong man to run a race."
(Psalm 19:5)

 # Oo

Opera, a type of entertainment in which the words of a drama are sung.

Marian Anderson gave concerts all over Europe and then returned to the United States and became the first black person to sing at the Metropolitan Opera.

"I will sing with the spirit, and I will sing with the understanding also." *(1Corinthians 14:15)*

Pencil Sharpener, a machine or tool for sharpening pencils.

John Lee Love invented the pencil sharpener in 1897.

". . .That a child may write them." (Isaiah 10:19)

Pp

Poet, a person who writes poetry.

Langston Hughes, one of the best-loved poets of America, wrote about the pleasures, joys, and sorrows of ordinary black people.

"For in him we live, and move, and have our being; as certain also of your own poets have said . . . ." (Acts 17:28)

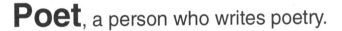

Simple's Uncle Sam

Goodbye Christ

The Weary Blues

Ballad of Ozzie Powell

Simple Takes a Wife

Quarterback, the football player who directs the offense of the team.

Doug Williams was an all-American quarterback for Grambling State University and then went on to play in the National Football League.

"Be strong and of good courage. . . ."
(1 Chronicles 28:20)

  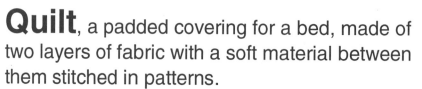

Quilt, a padded covering for a bed, made of two layers of fabric with a soft material between them stitched in patterns.

Harriet Powers was born into slavery in 1837 and died in 1911 a free woman. She is remembered for two of her quilts, preserved in museums, that were made using an appliqué technique typical of West Africa.

". . . And the pattern of it, according to all the workmanship thereof." (2 Kings 16:10)

Race-car Driver, one who competes in high-speed car races.

Willy T. Ribbs became the first African American to qualify for the Indianapolis 500.

"Let us run with patience the race that is set before us."
(Hebrews 12:1)

 # Rr

Runner, a person who competes in a foot race.

Florence Griffith Joyner won three gold medals and one silver medal at the 1988 Summer Olympic Games.

"Know ye not that they which run in a race run all, but one receiveth the prize?" *(1Corinthians 9:24)*

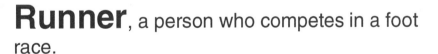

Scientist, a person who works in a science, especially a natural or physical science.

Charles Drew discovered how to separate plasma from whole blood and was responsible for setting up blood banks. Because plasma can be stored a long time and can be given to a person with any blood type, his discovery has saved many lives.

"For the life of the flesh is in the blood . . . ."
(Leviticus 17:11)

Skater, a person who skates on ice.

Debi Thomas became the first African American to win in the Winter Olympic Games when she won a bronze medal in figure skating in 1988.

"A gracious woman retaineth honor." (Proverbs 11:16)

Tennis, a game played on a rectangular court by two players using rackets to hit a ball over a low net.

Arthur Ashe was the first African American to win the international tennis tournament at Wimbledon.

"Do you see those who are skillful in their work?"
(Proverbs 22:29)

Tt

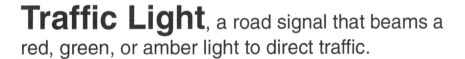

Traffic Light, a road signal that beams a red, green, or amber light to direct traffic.

Garrett A. Morgan invented the automatic three-way traffic light.

"...to give them light in the way wherein they should go."
(Nehemiah 9:12)

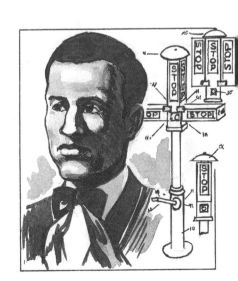

Ultraviolet, of the range of radiation wavelengths just beyond the violet in the visible spectrum.

George E. Carruthers designed the ultraviolet camera that was used in space to photograph the moon's surface.

"The LORD...giveth the sun for a light by day, and the ordinances of the moon and of the stars for a light by night." (Jeremiah 31:35)

Uu

Underground Railroad, a system that helped slaves to escape by moving them from one hiding place to another until they reached freedom in the North.

Harriet Tubman, an escaped slave, made nineteen courageous journeys into the Deep South and led over three hundred slaves to freedom.

"If the Son therefore shall make you free, ye shall be free indeed." (John 8:36)

Venturer, one who travels in spite of risks.

Matthew A. Henson, an African American who accompanied Admiral Peary to the North Pole, placed the American flag on the spot on April 7, 1909.

"Though I walk in the midst of trouble, thou wilt revive me." (Psalm 138:7)

Vv

Violin, a type of musical instrument that is played by drawing a bow across four strings.

Walter F. Craig was a violinist who organized Craig's Celebration Orchestra.

"Provide me now a man that can play well." (1 Samuel 16:17)

Watercolorist, a painter who paints with water-soluble pigments.

Lois Jones Pierre-Noel was a professor of art at Howard University from 1930 to 1977 and is known internationally for her award-winning paintings.

"A word fitly spoken is like apples of gold in pictures of silver." (Proverbs 25:11)

Ww

Writer, a person who writes, especially as an occupation; an author.

Maya Angelou has written poems and plays and is well-known for her autobiography, *I Know Why the Caged Bird Sings*, written in 1970.

"I come: in the volume of the book it is written of me . . . ." (Psalm 40:7)

Xavier University, an African American university in New Orleans that prepares students in the fields of pharmacy, pre-med, and engineering.

Nate "Sweetwater" Clifton, who attended Xavier University, became the first black player in the National Basketball Association when he was drafted by the New York Knicks in 1951.

"Seek ye first the kingdom of God . . . and all these things shall be added unto you." (Matthew 6:33)

X-ray, to photograph with a high-energy photon.

Frederick McKinley Jones developed refrigerated railroad cars and trucks and the portable x-ray machine.

"I may tell all my bones: they look and stare upon me." (Psalm 22:17)

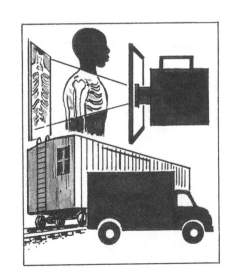

Yams, a sweet potato having reddish flesh.

George Washington Carver revolutionized southern agriculture by developing hundreds of products from peanuts and sweet potatoes.

"Thine hast planted them, yea, they have taken root: they grow, yea, they bring forth fruit . . . ." (Jeremiah 12:2)

 # Yy

Youth, the period of life between childhood and adulthood.

Mary McLeod Bethune founded a school for poor children in Florida, which became Bethune-Cookman College. Later she became an advisor to President Franklin Roosevelt as the director of the Negro Affairs Division of the National Youth Administration.

"I remember thee, the kindness of thy youth . . . ." (Jeremiah 2:2)

Zimbabwe, an African nation that was granted independence from Great Britain in 1980.

Randall Robinson founded TransAfrica, an organization of African Americans that has influenced United States foreign policy toward the countries of Africa.

"A land which the LORD thy God careth for . . . ."
(Deuteronomy 11:12)

Zz

Zoologist, a scientist who studies animals.

Geraldine Pittman Woods, a zoologist, has helped to develop college programs that increase minority participation in biomedical research and training.

"And God said, Let the earth bring forth the living creature after his kind, cattle and creeping things . . . ."
(Genesis 1:24)

Bibliography

Adams, Russell L. *Great Negroes Past and Present*, third edition. Chicago: Afro-Am Publishing Company, Inc., 1976.

African Americans: Voices of Triumph: Leadership. Alexandria, Va.: Time Life Books, 1993.

African Americans: Voices of Triumph: Perseverance. Alexandria, Va.: Time Life Custom Pub, 1993.

Carson, Ben. *Gifted Hands: The Ben Carson Story*. Grand Rapids: Zondervan Books, 1990.

Haskins, Jim. *Outward Dreams: Black Inventors and Their Inventions*. New York: Bantam Books, 1992.

Phelps, Shirelle, editor and William C. Matney, Jr., consulting editor. *Who's Who Among Black Americans, 1994—1995*. Detroit: Gale Research Inc., 1994.

Ploski, Harry A., and Brown, Jr., Roscoe C., editors. *Negro Almanac*. New York: Bellwether Publishing Co., 1967.

Ploski, Harry A., ed., with James Williams. *Reference Library of Black America, Vol. 4*. New York: Gale Research Inc., 1990.

Who's Who in America: Student Edition, 1989-1991, 4 vols. Marquis: New Providence, N.J., 1989.

Games

Question and Answer Game

For any size group or individual play.

Object of the game: To learn to identify names of African Americans with their accomplishments.

1. Use the cards to test knowledge of what was learned in the book. Either give the person's name from the card and ask for the associated accomplishment, or give the accomplishment and ask for the person's name.

2. You may use the cards as flash cards by covering the name at the bottom and holding the cards up for another person to try to correctly identify. This can also be an individual activity.

3. Refer to the book to read about those you don't remember.

Memory/Matching Game

For 4 to 6 players.

Object of the game: To match cards by alphabetical letter and to remember the location of matching cards in order to hold the most pairs at the end of the game.

1. Spread all the cards face down on the table so that they do not overlap.

2. The first player turns over any two cards. If the letters match, the player keeps them and turns over two more cards. If they match, the player continues drawing until the cards drawn do not match. If the cards do not match, they are placed face down on the table in the same position they were in, and that player's turn is ended.

3. The next player turns over two cards in an attempt to make a match, trying to remember which cards have previously been turned over so that he or she can use them to make a match. The turn continues until two cards are drawn that do not match.

4. The process is repeated until all the cards have been matched. The player with the most pairs wins.

5. If time permits, you may wish to share the names and accomplishments of the people on the cards, and then refer to the book for further information.

Treasure Chest (Go Fish)

For 3 to 6 players.

Object of the game: To get rid of all your cards by matching pairs of cards according to their alphabet letter. You may choose to match only uppercase letters with uppercase letters and the same for lowercase, or you may consider either form of the same letter a match.

1. Make sure the cards are mixed up well. Give seven cards to each player if you have three players. If you have four or more players, give five cards to each. Players do not pick up their cards until all have been handed out.

2. Spread the rest of the cards face down in the center of the players. This is the "treasure chest" pile to draw from.

3. Players now pick up and arrange the cards in their hands and place any matching sets of two face down in front of themselves.

4. The first player asks any other player for a card to match one in his or her hand. (For example: "Do you have a lowercase 'a'?") This player continues as long as other players have what he or she is looking for.

5. If no one has what the person is looking for, he or she then draws one card from the treasure chest and the turn is over.

6. Play continues until one person gets rid of all of his or her cards. That person is the winner.

About the Cards

One set of cards has been provided in this book. Card sets may be duplicated as needed for classroom use. The games included here require two sets; you may want to make more if you will have several groups playing at the same time. It is suggested that you photocopy the cards on heavier paper (book folds flat for easy copying) and then laminate them with clear plastic for greater durability. To separate cards, cut along the solid lines. For storage, consider baseball-card pocket holders or a container such as a file box.

a	**A**	**b**	**B**
Architect	**Astronaut**	**Baseball**	**Bicycle**
Julian Abele	Guion Stewart Bluford, Jr.	Jackie Robinson	I.R. Johnson
c	**C**	**d**	**D**
Church	**Composer**	**Director**	**Doctor**
George Liele	Thomas Andrew Dorsey	Oprah Winfrey	Ben Carson
e	**E**	**f**	**F**
Educator	**Electric Railway**	**Filmmaker**	**Fountain Pen**
Benjamin E. Mays	Granville T. Woods	John Singleton	William B. Purvis

g **General** Benjamin O. Davis, Sr.	**G** **Golf Tee** George F. Grant	**h** **Heart Surgeon** Daniel Hale Williams	**H** **Historian** Carter G. Woodson
i **Inventor** Jan Ernst Matzeliger	**I** **Ironing Board** Sarah Boone	**j** **Journalist** Ida B. Wells Barnett	**J** **Judge** Thurgood Marshall
k **Kentucky Derby** Jimmy Winkfield	**K** **Kwanzaa** Maulana Ron Karenga	**l** **Lawn Mower** J.A. Burr	**L** **Lawyer** Edith Sampson

m	**M**	**n**	**N**
Mathematician Benjamin Banneker	**Missionary** Lott Carey	**News Reporter** Ed Bradley	**Nobel Peace Prize** Dr. Martin Luther King, Jr.
o	**O**	**p**	**P**
Olympic Games Jesse Owens	**Opera** Marian Anderson	**Pencil Sharpener** John Lee Love	**Poet** Langston Hughes
q	**Q**	**r**	**R**
Quarterback Doug Williams	**Quilt** Harriet Powers	**Race-car Driver** Willy T. Ribbs	**Runner** Florence Griffith Joyner

s **Scientist** Charles Drew	**S** **Skater** Debi Thomas	**t** **Tennis** Arthur Ashe	**T** **Traffic Light** Garrett A. Morgan
u **Ultraviolet** George E. Carruthers	**U** **Underground Railroad** Harriet Tubman	**v** **Venturer** Matthew A. Henson	**V** **Violin** Walter F. Craig
w **Watercolorist** Lois Jones Pierre-Noel	**W** **Writer** Maya Angelou	**x** **Xavier University** Nate "Sweetwater" Clifton	**X** **X-ray** Frederick McKinley Jones

y	Y	z	Z
Yams George Washington Carver	**Youth** Mary McLeod Bethune	**Zimbabwe** Randall Robinson	**Zoologist** Geraldine Pittman Woods